Chinese Figure Painting for Beginners

Jia Xiangguo

Translated by Wen Jingen with Pauline Cherrett

FOREIGN LANGUAGES PRESS

First Edition 2007

Text by Jia Xiangguo
English translation by Wen Jingen with Pauline Cherrett
Designed by Cai Rong
Art by Jia Xiangguo, Sun Shuming and Wen Jingen

Chinese Figure Painting for Beginners

ISBN 978-7-119-04813-0
© 2007 by Foreign Languages Press
Published by Foreign Languages Press
24 Baiwanzhuang Road, Beijing, 100037, China
Home page: http://www.flp.com.cn
Email address: info@flp.com.cn
sales@flp.com.cn
Distributed by China International Book Trading Corporation
35 Chegongzhuang Xilu, Beijing 100044, China
P. O. Box 399, Beijing, China

Printed in the People's Republic of China

Contents

Translator's notes:

1. All illustrations in this book were executed and provided by the author unless otherwise stated. 写注明作者的图片均为本书作者所作。

2. To make this book more accessible for non-Chinese readers, the translator has extensively edited the original text, and added some illustrations. The translator, and not the author, is responsible for all errors accruing from the rewriting and rearrangement of the arts.

为适应外国读者需要，本书编译过程中对原作的图文做了一定改动。着粪续貂，在所难免；所生舛误，咎在译者。敬希作者及读者见谅。

Keep away from people who try to belittle your ambitions. Small people always do that, but the really great make you feel that you, too, can become great. — Mark Twain

Introduction

Wen Jingen

This is a manual specially prepared for non-Chinese readers. To make this book more approachable for them, as a translator, I have extensively edited the original text and have taken the liberty to add some illustrations. For a beginner, the technical side of the genre is important and the theoretical issues seem of little relevance. But once you engage yourself in Chinese painting — a tradition quite different from your own — you will sooner or later encounter issues that may bewilder you if you are totally unprepared. That is why I have offered some suggestions in this introduction.

Take the Challenge: Paint Your Model with Accuracy

To paint a live human figure is the most challenging task for an artist. To my way of thinking, the difficulty does not lie in the complexity of the human form, as the body of an animal, say a horse or tiger, is not much simpler. The task is challenging because your viewers may ask "Who is the person in your picture?" It is not likely they would ask the same question when viewing pictures of animals. In short, to paint a human figure is difficult because the audience expects more from figure painters. In fact, it is not very difficult to paint a human form — even school children without any special training can draw a figure in their own way, and primitive people painted many human figures in their caves. Yet it is difficult to paint the "whole" person of your model. In certain ancient cultures where people were not so critical of painters, or where an exact likeness was not expected, caricature-like figures executed in bold, dashing lines and colour patches were produced in abundance. But today, in the context of our time, most viewers expect to see a definite likeness of a certain person or persons in a figure painting.

The intimidating task makes many artists flinch. Not a few Chinese painters, especially those "literati" artists, shun this genre all their lives. Small wonder that trainee or amateur artists think they are not destined to be figure painters as they experience setbacks.

However it is a misconception to say that only "gifted" people can be figure painters. Experiences in contemporary art schools have proved that through step-by-step courses any student of average calibre can have a command of figure painting techniques. By honing one's eye-hand-mind co-ordination through constant practice, all budding artists can become figure painters!

First Step

Like people in other professions or hobbies, new figure painters need two things — ambition and skill. To keep your ambition focused is of the foremost importance. On the technical side, the basic skills for Chinese figure painting are more or less the same as those for a Western figure painter. If you have learned to draw human figures, congratulations! You are at a good starting point; otherwise I recommend that you study drawing first.

I say this because Chinese figure painting is a much-innovated tradition — far more than landscape or bird-and-flower. In the 20th century, the great realist painter and art educator Xu Beihong (1895-1953) emphasised drawing from life. He had a famous maxim: "Artists are not worthy being teachers (for artists)." He revolutionised

Admonitions of the Court Instructress to Palace Ladies (detail) by Gu Kaizhi. In our eyes, these well-proportioned figures cannot be likeness of particular people.

art education by adding drawing into the curriculum for all art students. This narrowed the gap between Western and Chinese figure painting. Xu's influence is ubiquitous in Chinese fine arts today. Another art educator Pan Tianshou (1897-1971) in his teaching stressed the copying of ancient works, but while asking students of bird-and-flower and landscape paintings to devote most of their time to copying, he too gave students of figure painting more time to draw from life at the early stage of study. It is clear that drawing from life is the foundation for successful figure painting, in China as well in the West.

In today's art nothing is sacrosanct. Different schools of art take a variety of approaches. As the goal of this book is to introduce realist figure painting skills, readers should ideally have some drawing experience. If, however, you intend to learn how to reproduce works of ancient masters, you should also study traditional brushwork and ink skills by copying from ancient works. In fact naturalistic drawing could hinder your command of ancient skills. Nowadays the pictures on fake handicrafts sold in roadside shops or stands are often betrayed by the use of correct anatomical presentation as taught in art schools today, but which was unknown to ancient Chinese painters.

Chinese Manners

Those who study Chinese art often encounter a problem — how "Chinese" is his or her painting? Using Chinese instruments is no guarantee for producing a painting in real Chinese style. As early as in the late 17th century European artists began to use Chinese ink (once erroneously known as the "Indian ink") and Chinese brushes, (James Ayres, *The Artist's Craft*, Phaidon, 1985) but their paintings did not look "Chinese". Over centuries Chinese painters have developed highly mature and sophisticated types of strokes. As in Chinese calligraphy, Chinese painters preferred neat and spontaneous strokes without retouching. The Chinese quality of a painting lies in, among other things, the special brushwork and ink application, and it takes time to master such skills.

In former times, Chinese artists used to learn brushwork skills by copying other, earlier artists' works and when they created a new painting they tried to match their images to the patterns they had learned. Compare the nose of the ladies in three paintings created in different periods of time by three different artists and you will see that a pattern was repeatedly used. Neat and beautiful as the "one-stroke" method is, it is no guarantee for a truthful representation.

Obviously, if one sticks to this type of neat stroke that refuses retouching, one is likely to achieve good brushwork at the expense of formal accuracy. Of course some masters can achieve accurate depiction and highly spontaneous brushwork, as shown in Xu Beihong's portrait. But it is impractical to expect a beginner to achieve this. To have a good grounding in figure painting, I strongly recommend the following principle — it is better to have loose brushwork than loose form.

I propose this because, as I have said before, Chinese figure painting is a revolutionised tradition. So, unlike Chinese landscape and bird-and-flower paintings whose basic brushwork is achievable through copying formulae, contemporary Chinese figure painting offers few ideas. To gain good brushwork, a figure painter also has to practise other genres of painting. This I will discuss later.

Jade Lady, from wall painting
of the Yongle Palace, Yuan
Dynasty (1271—1368)

Han Xizai's Nightly Feast (detail)
by Gu Hongzhong (10th century)

The Moon Goddess by Tang Yin (1470 — 1523)

Those paintings were created by different masters. Note that the nose in all of them was executed with the same single hooked stroke.

Portrait of Li Yinquan by Xu Beihong (1895 — 1953)

This masterpiece is admired for accurate depiction and spontaneous brushwork.

Likeness & Beyond

A hackneyed issue in Chinese art theory is which one of "formal resemblance" and "spiritual resemblance" is important. There are mountains of views on this topic. Many Chinese art theorists hold that spiritual resemblance can be achieved only through formal resemblance. Nevertheless some literati artists claim that they disdain the formal resemblance achieved by meticulous depiction. They insist that spiritual resemblance comes from their mysterious communication with nature. The dispute has been going on for centuries and there is no sign that a consensus will be reached. If you delve into these debates, it is likely that you will be more puzzled than enlightened. I am in no position to make any judgement on this controversy. I would just like to put forward a few points for readers to consider:

1. Ancient Chinese art history and criticism is heavily biased. Most written documents on art were written by officials / scholars. They were literarily well educated but most of them lacked strict training in painting. This was especially true during the latter phase of the Imperial China. As China's leading painter Xu Beihong pointed out, "Artists who mean to cover up their errors always put forward their own theories. The more sophisticated the theory, the weaker the art". (*Benteng Chi Fu Jian*, [Galloping on a Foot-long Picture], Tianjin, Baihua Wenyi Chubanshe, 2000, p. 252) The literati painters played up their amateurism and played down professional painting techniques. If we do not believe the Emperor's new clothes, we can find that human figures in literati artists' works are poorly executed. Just as Wang Shixiang says in his epilogue to *Introduction to Painting* (Huishi Zhimeng 绘事指蒙), "Men of letters belittled artisans or craftsmen and paid little attention to their works and experiences. Those scholars claimed that they disdained to do as the artisans did, but in fact they

were ignorant and incapable in this field." (*Chinese Folk Painting Formulae* [Zhongguo Minjian Huajue 中国民间画诀], Beijing Gongyi Meishu Chubanshe, 2003, p. 221)

2. Chinese literati painters knew more than their hands could perform. Ancient Chinese art theorists were aware that it was important to present the volume of depicted objects. Guo Ruoxu in his *Tuhua Jianwen Zhi* (Records of Seen and Heard-of Pictures 图画见闻志) criticised three errors in pictorial representation. One of the three was "...to present objects flat, unable to present them in the round" (……状物平扁，不能圆浑). If you look at the self-portrait by an established master with an innocent eye, you can see the human form is rather flat.

Yet this painting has been praised for "graphically portraying the pride, aloofness and refined air of Jin Nong the supercilious commoner". (*Immortal Chinese*

Self-portrait by Jin Nong (1687 — 1763)

Note the flat human form

Painting [Zhongguo Chuanshi Ming Hua 中国传世名画], Zhengzhou, Haiyan Chubanshe, 2002, p. 294). Can you see this in the picture?

The art critic Rao Ziran (1312 — 1365) listed artists' twelve "errors", one of which was the "humpbacked figure". Yet due to ignorance of human anatomy, this error was not corrected. These distorted figures appeared frequently in Chinese painting.

Another masterwork is a "classical" portrait of a scholar by the name of Yang Zhuxi.

In art historical documents this portrait has been repeatedly praised for its vividness and resemblance to the model. A recent commentary is found in the website of the Palace Museum, Beijing (http://www.dpm. org.cn/China/default.asp). It says the portrait displays Yang's

Four Pleasures of Nan Lusheng (detail)
by Chen Hongshou, Yan Zhan and Chen Zi, 1469

Episode from Historical
Stories (detail)
by Wu Li (1632 — 1718)

Wang Yuanqi Viewing Chrysanthemum (detail)
by Yu Zhiding (1647 — 1716)

Immortal Liu Hai Playing with a Toad
by Min Zhen (b. 1730)

Bat Flying from the Sky
by Ren Yi (1840 — 1895)

Note the humpbacked figures in those masters' works on this and previous two pages.

personality, and is a "close resemblance of the model's expression" (神情毕肖).

Portrait of Yang Zhuxi by Wang Yi and Ni Zan, 1363

It is interesting to compare the above comment with James Cahill's on the same painting: "Chinese descriptions of the painting praise the portraitist's capturing of Yang Zhuxi's 'uprightness and respectfulness'. Although this is true, we should note also that the characterization is not accomplished (as Chinese theorists insist) by some penetrating portrayal of the face that reveals the subject's inner nature — the face is bland and expressionless — but, as usual in Chinese portraits, by stance, attributes, and setting, all of which function as signs to be read by the knowing viewer."* (*3000 Years of Chinese Painting*, Yale University Press and Foreign Languages Press, 1997, p. 154)

Which of them is closer to the mark? Pass your own judgement.

---

* If we compare this painting with Xu Beihong's portrait, we will know a good portrait does not rely on setting or symbolic vocabulary.

3. It is clear that formal resemblance is not the ultimate goal of portraiture. A person's photographs undoubtedly all look like him or her. But still we can feel that some pictures present the person's "character" while others look dull and insipid. In Chinese art critics' jargon, the former shows a "formal resemblance" together with a "spiritual resemblance" and the latter merely shows the formal version. In other words, in portraiture we expect something beyond a likeness.

If we compare a good photograph and a bad one, we will notice that the former captures subtleties in a person's mien: a hardly noticeable curl of the lips, a faint gleaming in the pupil, a subconscious tension in certain muscles in the face, a barely undetectable twitch of the eyebrows — it is these subtleties that contribute to the uniqueness of a person's "character". It goes without saying that only through a realistic rendering of a person's form can his or her unique personal character be revealed. One can hardly imagine that a picture which bears no resemblance in form can manifest such subtleties.

Artists often ask the question, "If I don't mean to produce a portrait of a certain person, why should I bother to do a realistic representation?" My answer is — in our time with state-of-the-art photography, realistic figure painting no longer serves as identification of certain persons as it did in olden times. But realistic representation is the vehicle for expression of the uniqueness of each individual person, and it is this uniqueness that makes many outstanding figure paintings immortal. Mona Lisa is not a beautiful lady, she is simply "herself". If you want to endow each of your figures with special charm, you have to resort to naturalistic depiction. Jiang Caiping (b. 1934), an accomplished Chinese figure painter, claims that she never fabricates a figure in her painting. (Jiang Caiping, *Techniques to Use Chinese Painting Tools*

[Zhongguohua Cailiao Yingyong Jifa 中国画材料应用技法], Shanghai Renmin Meishu Chubanshe, 1999, p.74) If we examine a master's successful and less successful works, we will find that in the former each figure is different from the others while in the latter they have similar faces. This convinces us from the negative side how important faithful depiction is in figure painting.

It seems that this point of view is refutable on the grounds that many master painters create unrealistic figures. And it is true that many ancient art works of disproportionate human figures have no less appeal than average modern paintings of well-proportioned figures. To understand this phenomenon we should consider the social contexts of artistic activities. In various cultures during a certain period of time the audience did not expect much accuracy in figure painting. On the other hand, many modern artists deliberately pursue surrealistic effect in their artistic creation. But if we examine Pablo Picasso's paintings and drawings we find some of his severely distorted images still bear resemblance to the sitters. Thus we can say that some ancient figure paintings present less than a likeness (though this is often compensated with the artists' attainments in other aspects, which are absent in many "avant-garde" artists' works), and some modern masters present more than a likeness. For them, naturalistic depiction is still a basis for their work.

For a beginner of figure painting, to hone the ability in realistic depiction is a rewarding practice no matter what style or theory he or she will uphold in his or her later career or hobby.

Stylisation — "a Brand in the Market but Not a Blessing for Artists"

As an artist masters the language of art, his or her art tends to become stylised. This is hardly avoidable. Dante Gabriel Rossetti's portraits are recognisable by the high-cheek boned long faces with squarish lips. In the market, stylised images make a brand. Art dealers hope artists will continually provide saleable goods, and goods with a brand are saleable. Once an artist makes a name for himself or herself, his or her creation tends to be directed (or even controlled) by the market. He or she is asked to reproduce stereotyped images. If an artist does not pursue money but pursues art, he or she must avoid this pitfall. French artist Jean Corot and Chinese artist Huang Binhong seldom sold their paintings during their lifetimes. Those artists with unrelenting endeavour for perfection set good examples for later artists.

However retentive an artist's visual memory is, he or she cannot reproduce all the physiognomic subtleties of many people from memory. (It is a myth that 5th-century painter Xie He could paint a lifelike portrait from his memory after just a glance at the model. No extant work corroborates such records.) To shake off stereotypes, an artist has to observe life attentively and always approach life as a new hand.

Be an All-round Painter

When a student asked John Singer Sargent how to become a great portrait painter he replied, "if he is only a portrait painter, he is nobody. Try to become a painter first and then apply your knowledge to a special branch." Almost all good Chinese painters are calligraphers. As you are learning Chinese painting but may not know Chinese calligraphy, I would suggest that you learn Chinese bird-and-flower painting as well. In bird-and-flower painting the requirement for accurate forms is not as exacting as in figure painting, but at the same time, the artist can give full rein to brushwork and ink. Training in the application of these skills is crucially important.

A Glimpse into Chinese Figure Painting Through the Dynasties

Chinese figure painting has a long history. During prehistoric times, many pictures of animals and human figures were chiselled onto rocks. The main mode of expression in those "paintings" was line. The simple lines vividly portrayed the primitive tribes' hunting and dancing. On those rock paintings black, white and red mineral pigments were applied. Modern archaeological findings include figure paintings dating back to the New Stone Age. Most of the figures of that time have been discovered on pottery and other daily use utensils.

At an early stage Chinese civilization was noted for its patriarchal clan system that had taken the place of primitive Shamanism. During that era, the worship of ancestors had replaced the earlier pantheism. The period from the 22nd to the 3rd centuries BC was China's "Bronze Age". Simple and immature human figures have been found on bronze ritual utensils.

Human face and fish pattern on pottery, 5,000 — 3,000 BC

Dancers on pottery, 3,000 — 2,000 BC

With the division of labour when humans entered the class society, professional painters soon emerged. Historical documents record that the prime minister of the first king of the Shang Dynasty (c.1600 — c. 1100 BC) admonished the king by showing him the pictures of nine virtuous ancient rulers. An anecdote says that Confucius once saw the portraits of good and bad prehistoric rulers on the wall of a palace. Figure painting often served political purposes so it was highly regarded by the ruling class, and it therefore flourished.

Earliest paintings on silk discovered so far, date back to the period 8th century BC — 2nd century AD. From these paintings we can see that early Chinese painters had been able to produce human figures with accurate anatomical proportion. After a long evolution silk painting became the scroll for artistic appreciation.

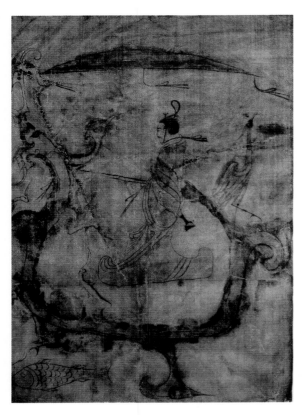

Dragon rider by unknown artist during the Warring States period (475 — 221 BC)

The T-shaped silk painting unearthed from the Tomb of Marquise Dai in Changsha

The painting was used as a "soul flag" - a funeral object used during the Han Dynasty (206 BC — AD 220). The painting is divided into a top, middle and a bottom. The top displays the paradise in Heaven. The three round designs (one on the right with a bird in it) are the sun, the moon and a human-headed and snake-bodied deity symbolizing life. The middle part shows the world, with the figure as the tomb occupant. Mythical animals and birds are also found in this depiction of the human world. On the bottom is the nether world, the world of souls, where a giant supports the earth on his head. These three worlds are linked together by two winding dragons.

Goddess of River Luo by Gu Kaizhi (active A.D. 317 — 420)

This painting is based on a literary masterpiece "Rhapsody on the Goddess of River Luo" (Luo Shen Fu) by the poet Cao Zhi (AD 192 — 232). The rhapsody relates how he met with the goddess on River Luo, where they fell in love and conveyed their feelings to each other. However, due to the "barrier between human and divine worlds", they could not have intimate contact and thus they departed in tears, broken-hearted. The detail of the painting shows the goddess and her retinue riding away in her chariot carried by mythical beasts (bottom) and the poet in a high cabin of a ship gazing at the goddess (top).

From the 3rd to the 6th centuries, Chinese figure painting became mature. It was a time when Buddhism spread amongst all social strata. Apart from paintings with themes drawn from history and real life, artists also created Buddhist images and pictures illustrating stories from Buddhist scriptures. None of the original paintings have survived — all paintings attributed to artists of that date are copies done by later artists. However, archaeologists have discovered wall paintings in tombs from that period.

Paintings of that time are finely delineated and coloured; the line is rhythmical and smooth. Historians compared the line to "silk thread spun by spring silkworms".

This period also witnessed the maturing of art theory. The artist and art historian Xie He put forward his "Six Canons" (liu fa 六法) of painting. The six canons were:

1. Representing the bearing and vigour (of the depicted person);
2. Building structure through brushwork;
3. Depicting the forms of things as they are;
4. Appropriate colouring;
5. Composition;
6. Transcribing and copying.

Originally, the first canon dealt with representation of human figure. Later it extended to the representation of landscape and other motifs, and its interpretation was changed to "**creating a lifelike tone and atmosphere**". These "canons" have been upheld ever since they were put forward, but the interpretation and translation of them have been heatedly debated.

The period AD 618 — 907, known as the Tang dynasty in China, was a time of unprecedented prosperity and power. Religious arts became secularised. During that time the artistic style inherited from previous dynasties (noted for fine line and meticulous depiction) was called "fine line style" (miti 密体 [體]). *Rulers of Past Dynasties* (历[歷]代

帝王图[圖]) may serve as an example of the "fine line style". Beside this style there appeared the "sparsely stroked style" (shuti 疏体 [體]) initiated by the master figure painter Wu Daozi. Unfortunately no authentic work of this master is extant — the few paintings attributed to him are spurious. According to historical documents, his strokes were dashing, sweeping and with breaks in the brushwork. It is believed that Wu Daozi drew on the art introduced from the western region of

Rulers of Past Dynasties by Yan Liben (d. AD 673)

China and Central Asia. "Heavenly King Delivering a Baby" has been attributed to him.

Other "fine line style" masters include Zhou Fang, Zhang Xuan and Sun Wei.

Sage Painter (hua sheng 画圣[畫聖])

Wu Daozi has been honoured as the "sage painter" by Chinese people. He created 300 wall murals and many paintings on scrolls. He worked rapidly and his brushwork was vigorous and forceful, human figures created by him were passionate and imposing. He must have been an excellent realist painter, for a historical record has it that he once modelled a Bodhisattva on his own visage.

Vimalakirti — attributed to Wu Daozi

Spring Outing of Lady Guoguo (detail) by Zhang Xuan

Scholars (detail) by Zhou Wenju ▶
(AD 917 — 975)

During the period of the Five Dynasties (AD 907 — 960) China was in disarray. This period produced master figure painters like Gu Hongzhong (c. AD 910 — 980) and Guan Xiu (AD 832 — 912). The latter's paintings are noted for the grotesque-looking arhats. It is said he created them according to what he had seen in his dreams.

Arhats by Guan Xiu (attrib)

Fairies (detail) by Ruan Gao

Chinese Figure Painting for Beginners

Night Feast of Han Xizai (detail) by Gu Hongzhong

Han Xizai was an important court minister of the Southern Tang Dynasty (one of the Five Dynasties) but he was mistrusted by the sovereign. Because the weak Southern Tang regime felt threatened by a stronger regime in the northern China, the Southern Emperor strengthened his supervision over officials of a northern origin. At one time he intended to appoint Han Xizai as his prime minister, but did not quite trust him. Having been an official for many years, the worldly-wise Han Xizai clearly knew the emperor's intention. He did not mean to stay in officialdom, and under such circumstances, he showed an indifferent attitude towards political life. In his private life, he indulged in the entertainment of dancers and singers, so as to divert his colleagues' attention. Believing that Han Xizai really led a loose life, the emperor who "felt sorry for corruption of a talent" tried to persuade him "to reform" by way of a painting. The emperor dispatched the artist Gu Hongzhong (another version says Zhou Wenju) to Han's house to watch what he was doing. The artist committed Han's nightly, uproarious and debauched feasting to his memory, painted it and submitted the painting to the emperor.

In the Song Dynasty (960 — 1279) Chinese figure painting reached a higher level of perfection thanks to the installation of the royal painting academy in the imperial court. A large number of good figure painters were recruited into the academy. The imperial court enlisted artists to serve the interests of the ruling group, which had the effect of accelerating the development of figure painting. Zhao Ji (1082-1135), the emperor Huizong, was himself a virtuoso and an outstanding artist — one of his masterpieces was "Listening to the Zither *Qin*". Apart from drawing themes from history, artists of that time turned their eyes to the rural life. As a result, peasants, woodcutters, fishermen and herdsmen found their way into art works. Figure painters also borrowed techniques from landscape painting and made the background of their figures more beautiful. Zhang Zeduan created the panoramic scroll "Riverside Scene at Qingming Festival" that presented the capital city in its heyday. In his "Picking Vetch" Li Tang (1066 — 1150) combined the techniques of meticulous delineation and freestyle brushwork. Liang Kai was the well known, early master of freehand figure painting.

Poet Li Bai Chanting by Liang Kai

Vendor by unknown artist

Listening to the Zither *Qin* (detail) by Zhao Ji

Riverside Scene at Qingming Festival 清明上河图 （圖）(detail) by Zhang Zeduan

The horizontal scroll shows the scene in spring along the Bianhe River which travelled through the capital city during the Northern Song Dynasty. The artist's dates are unknown but we do know he was active somewhere between A.D. 1111 and 1125; other than this little is known about his life. In 1127 the northern China was occupied by the Nüzhen (Jurchen, later known as Manchu) people and the Song Dynasty court fled south. The artist was one of the refugees fleeing from the north. It is said that he created the painting from his memory of the once prosperous capital city in the north.

Riverside Scene at Qingming Festival (detail) by Zhang Zeduan

Picking Vetch (detail)
by Li Tang

Picking Vetch by Li Tang

This painting presents an anecdote about two noble brothers who lived at the end of the Shang Dynasty period (1600 — 1100 BC). The last king of the dynasty was cruel and debauched. The lord of a fiefdom launched an armed revolt against the rule of the cruel king. When the rebelling lord was about to set off, the noble brothers tried in vain to stop him. The rebels soon took over the capital, put an end to the Shang Dynasty and established a new dynasty. The brothers disdained to become subjects of the new regime. They swore never to eat the grain of the new rulers, so they entered the Shouyang Mountains (in present-day Shanxi Province) and lived on vetch. A village woman saw them and said, "You refuse to eat the new regime's grain, but the herb belongs to it too." On hearing this, the brothers gave up eating the wild plant as well and in the end they died of hunger.

Portrait of Kublai Khan by unknown artist

In 1279 China fell to the Mongols who established the Yuan Dynasty (1279 — 1368). Under the Mongolian rule the Han-ethnic intellectuals were suppressed and stayed in the bottom strata of society. Many scholars became apathetic to reality and turned their attention to landscape and plants. Figure painters of this time created many Buddhist or Daoist figures and portraits.

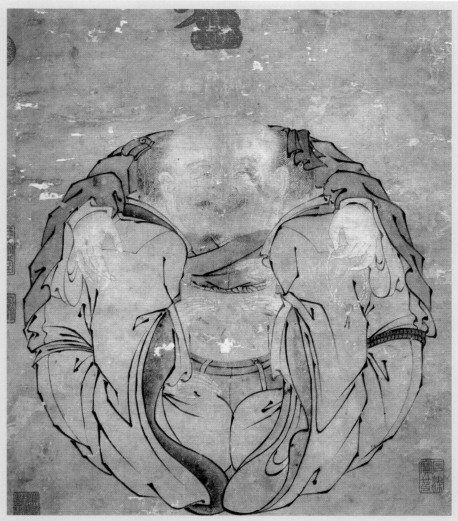

Picture of Harmony

This painting painted by Zhu Jianshen, the emperor Xianzong (r. 1465 —
1522), is enigmatic. At the first glance it appears to be one person, but at
a close observation it turns out to be three men merged into one. The
right part of the head wears a Confucian scholar's kerchief, the middle
part shows the shaved pate of a Buddhist monk and the left part has
Daoist headgear. The picture is symbolism of union of Confucianism,
Buddhism and Daoism.

This portrait of the scientist Xu Guangqi (1562 — 1633) by an unknown artist, shows the co-translator of Euclid's *Elements* (the other translator being the Italian missionary Matteo Ricii) and illustrates the achievement scored by Chinese artists in portraiture during the Ming Dynasty.

瞻髮圖

老蓮洪綬畫於

靜者軒

Washing Hair in Wine
by Chen Hongshou

The innovative artist Chen Hongshou (usually known by his style name Chen Laolian, 1598 — 1652) studied paintings of former times and incorporated what he learned from them in his creation. Human figures in his later works were rather grotesque but his brushwork was simple and refined.

Important progress was made by figure painters in late 14th century to early 17th century - they developed the freestyle figure painting, chiefly executed in ink.

Donkey Rider by Zhang Lu (1464 -1538)

Portrait by unknown artist

When did scholars began to engage themselves in producing paintings?

Huang Yue (Qing Dynasty) says, "In the ancient times drawing and painting were done by artisans. Since the Han Dynasty (206 BC — AD 220) fine pieces of painting have been created by men of letters." When these scholars and officials took up Chinese painting, it came to possess a more literary flavour. Since the Song Dynasty (AD 960 — 1279), ink painting became the mainstream of Chinese painting, with new forms and styles surfacing.

Emperor Qianlong on
Inspection (detail)
by Giuseppe Castiglione

Chinese figure painting during the Qing Dynasty (1644 — 1911) became more popular. There were two groups of figure painters. One group of artists worked for the imperial court and they triumphed in portraiture, the other worked outside of the imperial court where their artistic creation was noted for anti-traditional ideology. An important figure in the early Qing court was the Italian Jesuit missionary Giuseppe

Castiglione (1688-1766, Chinese name: Lang Shining). An all-around artist, he created many figures, horses and plants. His paintings incorporated the naturalistic depiction skills of the West with Chinese tradition, exerting a deep influence on Chinese court art.

Since 1840 China was increasingly exposed to the influence of Western thought. Many artists gathered in Shanghai and formed the

Female Immortal Ma Gu Presenting Longevity Peaches by Ren Xun (1835 — 1893)

Portrait of a Low-ranking Official by Ren Yi (1840 — 1895)

Shanghai School. Of the many masters, Ren Yi (1840 — 1895, alternatively known as Ren Bonian), scored the greatest achievement in portraiture. Incorporating techniques borrowed from the European art, he excelled in the human figure as well as in bird-and-flower painting. In terms of realistic depiction, brushwork or aesthetics, he brought Chinese figure painting to an unprecedented height.

In the early 20th century many Chinese artists went abroad and studied techniques of drawing, oil painting and block printing in Japan and Europe. They introduced Western art skills into Chinese painting and reformed traditional Chinese art. Xu Beihong (1895 — 1953), a great protagonist of realist art plus the marriage of Western and Chinese techniques, epitomised his art theory in his portraiture. Jiang Zhaohe's "Refugees" presented human figures by depicting the muscles and bone joints with traditional Chinese ink and brushwork.

In the latter half of the 20th century Chinese artists delved into reality and experienced the real social life. Their figure paintings display the mentality of their contemporaries. Many outstanding artists with a solid grounding in traditional techniques and naturalistic depiction emerged.

Since 1980s the Western avant-garde arts have exerted an influence on Chinese arts. Affected by contemporary foreign cultures, a number of Chinese artists turned their eyes from real life to the art itself, exploring the expressive potential of the ink. By borrowing Western expressionist practice and theories, they have been trying to create new forms and methods.

Portrait of Tagore by Xu Beihong (1895 — 1953) ▶

Refugees (detail) by Jiang Zhaohe (1904 — 1986); the painting presents the miserable
lives of Chinese people during the Japanese occupation in the 1930s and 1940s.

Washers' Night Song (detail) by Lin Fan (b. 1931)

Four Generations by Liu Wenxi (b. 1933)

Great writer Pu Songling by Ma Zhensheng (b. 1939)

Small Guests by Liu Guohui (b. 1940)

A Glimpse into Chinese Figure Painting Through the Dynasties   55

Dai Ethnic Teacher by Wu Shanming (b. 1941)

Tools

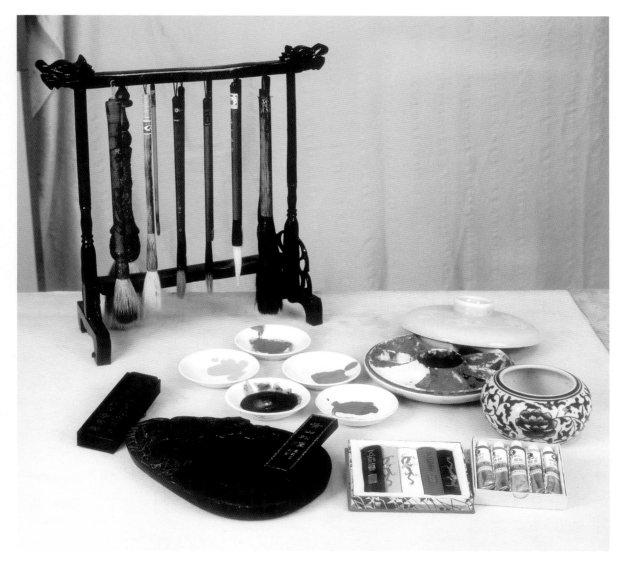

Photograph by Sun Shuming

The brush

The brush for Chinese painting is quite different from the brush for oil painting. The former has a pointed tip while the latter has a flat tip. The former is mainly for painting lines while the latter is primarily for spreading colours on canvas. Manipulating the brush in different ways produces the various strokes in Chinese painting.

Stiff-fibre brushes: Such brushes are made from hair of hare, weasel, or badger. There are about ten varieties of such brushes including *yi wen* 衣纹(紋) (clothing fold), *ye jin* 叶(葉)筋 (leaf vein), *lan zhu* 兰(蘭)竹 (orchid and bamboo), *shu hua* 书画(書畫) (calligraphy and painting), and *shan shui* 山水 (landscape). They are brushes for painting lines. The size of the brush is determined by the size of stroke desired.

Soft-fibre brushes: These brushes are mainly used to apply colour and produce dotted strokes. But they can also be used to paint lines. They are made of goat hair so they are called *yang hao* 羊毫 (goat's hair).

Mix-fibre brushes: Such brushes are made of mixed hairs, namely, stiff and soft fibres. They are neither very stiff nor very soft, so they are good tools for beginners. The major varieties are *da baiyun* 大白云(雲) (large white cloud), *zhong baiyun* 中白云(雲) (medium white cloud) and *xiao baiyun* 小白云(雲))(small white cloud), *xie zhao* 蟹爪 (crab's claw) and others.

In terms of the length of the brush fibres, brushes can be divided into long-fibre brushes and short-fibre brushes. Various painters have different preferences. You may try them all and find the brushes that suit you best.

Choosing a good brush

A good brush should have a straight shaft and fibres that have "four virtues": sharp pointed, flush, circular and resilient.

• Sharp pointed: when the brush tip is wet, it is sharply pointed;

good   bad

• Flush: when the brush tip is pressed flat, the end of the fibres form a straight line;

good

bad

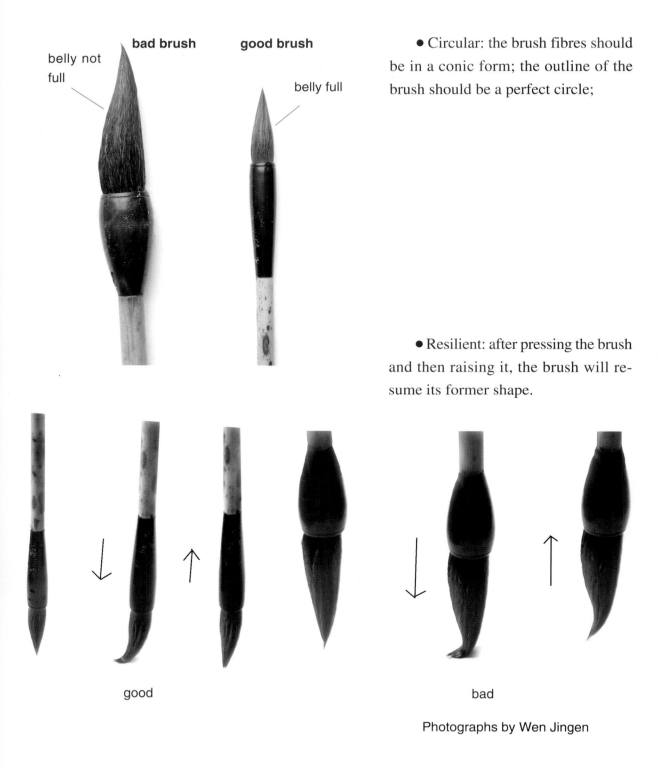

bad brush **good brush**

belly not full

belly full

- Circular: the brush fibres should be in a conic form; the outline of the brush should be a perfect circle;

- Resilient: after pressing the brush and then raising it, the brush will resume its former shape.

good

bad

Photographs by Wen Jingen

Using a new brush

If the fibres in the tip of a new brush are not glued together, just start using it. First wet the brush thoroughly in clean water, squeeze out the water, and then load it with ink and apply it to the paper.

If however a new brush has a glued tip (the fibres are sealed with alum or resin for the purpose of safe transportation), you can dip the brush in half a cup of water. Leave it in the water for a while and the alum or resin in the tip will be removed. You can now use it.

Always stroke the brush across a palette, tile or the lid of the ink stone to make sure all fibres lie adjacent to each other and a good point is formed.

If after stroking your brush, you still find surplus liquid in the brush; remove this by stroking the brush on a piece of absorbent tissue paper.

Washing your brush

After using, you must wash your brush. Then you can leave it horizontally it to dry. Still better, hang it tip downwards on a brush hanger and leave to dry. You must straighten and smooth the hairs in the brush, otherwise the fibres will dry in a tangle and the brush will not perform well.

Photograph by Sun Shuming

Ink

Ink is indispensable in Chinese painting. It plays a more important role than colour. A Chinese painting can be uncoloured, but it cannot be executed without using ink.

In former times, all Chinese artists used ink-sticks — the best ink sticks are produced in Anhui Province and hence the name *hui mo* 徽墨.

Some ink sticks are made from soot collected by burning pine wood — hence the name "pine soot ink" (*songyan* 松烟[煙]). Others are made from soot collected by burning oil (mainly tung oil) and hence the name "oil soot ink" (*youyan* 油烟[煙]). The latter is more lustrous than the former.

NB: Cheap ink sticks available in the market nowadays are neither "pine soot" nor "oil soot" ink sticks. They are by-products of the petro-chemical industry. Do not use such ink sticks for Chinese painting.

To produce ink, put water onto an ink stone, hold the ink stick vertically, press it lightly and move in a circle to grind it until the water becomes dark black. Do not put too much water onto the ink stone to start with. If you want to produce more ink, add water several times — a small amount each time. There is an old saying that "in rubbing an ink stick one acts like a sick man", meaning one must be patient and not exert too much effort.

Bottled ink has a shorter history. Many Chinese artists today use bottled ink, however, some artists insist on using traditional ink sticks because bottled ink produces fewer shades than ink sticks.

Photograph by Sun Shuming

Ink has "five colours" 墨分五彩

Diluted with different amount of water, ink can produce different shades. Usually art theorists grade the ink in five shades: in a descending order, they are: the dried-up ink (extremely dark, with no water mixed), dark, strong, light and pale (little ink mixed with large amount of water). Another version of this theory gives the following ink shades: dark, light, dry, wet and strong inks. Some art theorists add "white" to the five and change ink shades into six. In fact with different amounts of water mixed in, ink can have far more shades than five or six.

Illustration by Wen Jingen

Ink stone

The ink stone is for grinding the ink stick. It is also for holding the ground ink and for stroking the brush fibres so as to make them straight and adjacent to each other. An ink stone may be made of only one piece of stone (or other material), or with a lid (of the same material as the base or of wood). Nowadays many artists use bottled ink instead of an ink stick, so the ink stone is not as important as it used to be, but bottled ink cannot produce the pitch-black shade. When dried-up ink is needed, put some ink from the bottle onto an ink stone and grind an ink stick into it to produce extremely dry, dark ink. After using this, you must wash your ink stone clean.

Choose a good ink stone. Touch the ink stone with your hand; if the stone feels soft and smooth but not slippery, it is good. Famous ink stones include those from Duanxi, Guangdong Province, hence the name *duan yan* 端砚(硯), those from Wuyuan, Jiangxi Province (formerly part of Shexian, Anhui Province, hence the name *she yan* 歙砚[硯]), those from Taohe River, Gansu Province, hence the name *tao yan* 洮砚(硯), and others. A baked sedimentary-clay version of an ink stone has been used too.

Some ink stones are exquisitely designed, carved and ornamented, or are made of expensive materials like jade. They are more handicraft articles than artists' instruments.

Photograph by Wen Jingen

Paper and silk

The oldest Chinese paintings found so far were on silk. Paper emerged about two thousand years ago. Paper is cheaper than silk, but after the introduction of paper, silk remained in use and did not give up its predominance to paper until six hundred years ago. Nowadays most Chinese painters and calligraphers use a "Xuan paper". It is so named because it was believed to be originally produced in Xuancheng, Anhui Province. But some Xuan papers may be made in vicinity of Xuancheng or simply made using the same materials and procedure. There are no less than 60 varieties of "Xuan paper".

Xuan paper is not the only paper for Chinese painting. Other papers like *pi zhi* ("bark paper" 皮纸 , a tough paper made from bast fibre of the mulberry tree) can be used too.

Roughly, Chinese painting has two major styles. The meticulous style *gong bi* 工笔(筆) and free style *xie yi* 写(寫)意. In the same way, Xuan paper and silk fall into two categories, sized and unsized. Sized paper is more durable and stands repeated application of ink and colour. The unsized paper is absorbent and usually used for free style painting.

Some artists experiment with other papers e.g. watercolour paper. But water-resistant paper with a slippery surface like the paper used in photocopying is no good for Chinese painting.

Silk, once the major medium of painting, now has given way to paper. Some meticulous-style painters, however, still use sized silk to produce paintings in brilliant colours. In ancient times, artists would size the silk themselves; nowadays ready sized silk is available.

Colours

Chinese colours fall into two categories, "stone colour" (mineral pigments) and "herbal colour" (vegetable pigments). The former are body colours and the latter, transparent colours. Azurite, malachite, cinnabar, vermilion, ochre, gold powder, silver powder, and zinc white (in place of lead powder used long ago, which tended to turn dark with passage of time) are mineral colours; rattan yellow, indigo, and rouge

Colours and palette, photograph by Sun Shuming

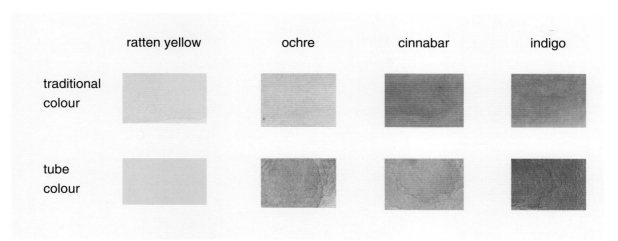

	ratten yellow	ochre	cinnabar	indigo
traditional colour				
tube colour				

by Wen Jingen

are vegetable colours. Traditional Chinese colours come in powder form. Some stone colours should be ground before using and dissolved in hot water with glue or alum.

You can also buy tube colours in stationery or art shops. These colours, like watercolour or gouache, are rather handy — you need not grind them or mix them with glue or alum. Nowadays many artists like using tube colours, but be aware that such paints are not genuine Chinese colours — they can produce quite different effects when applied on paper or silk. The traditional rattan yellow is more transparent than the tube version, traditional indigo is less "brilliant" than the tube indigo. Tube colours are chemical products while the traditional colours for Chinese painting are natural. Traditional Chinese colours are not as brilliant as chemical colours, but they are durable and do not fade or discolour with the elapse of time.

Other equipment

Palettes used by Chinese painters are made of porcelain. Some artists nevertheless like to use separate dishes instead of a palette especially when producing large paintings.

Painting felt is needed if you paint on unsized paper. Without a piece of felt or other absorbent material to cushion your paper, the ink and colour will run through the paper onto the table, then will come back to the paper and blot your strokes.

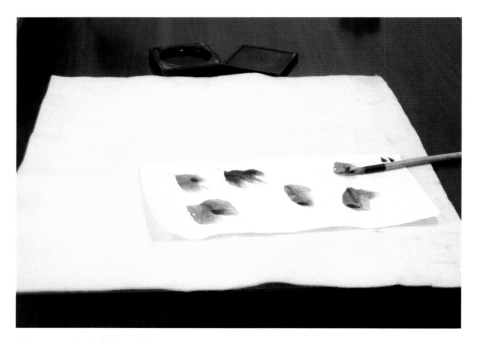

Photograph by Wen Jingen

You also need bowls or pots to contain water for washing your brushes. If you do not have specially made washing bowls, any wide-mouthed bottle or bowl will do.

Chinese artists often sign their works with one or more seal imprints, plus an inscription. Apart from serving as signature, seal prints also keep the composition of a painting in balance. Likewise, a seal imprint out of place will put the composition out of balance. That is why many artists contemplate a while before they impress the seal onto the paper. You can also impress your seal onto a spare piece of paper and move it around on the painting to assess the best position before applying the seal to your work.

Seals are made of stone, jade, horn or metal. Seals cut in jade, horn or metal are expensive and being hard materials do not allow the seal carver's individual creativity to show. Stone, on the other hand, tends to keep the carver's personal cutting style — that is why Chinese calligraphers and painters like using seals cut from stone. You may ask a seal carver to carve seals for you — or if you know Chinese "seal script", you can try to carve a seal stone for yourself. Usually red (cinnabar) seal paste is used.

Photograph by Sun Shuming

Seal script 篆书(書)

The so-called "seal script" Chinese characters are so named because today they are used in seals. But two thousand years ago such script was used in all forms of documents, not only in seals. Compare some seal script characters with those in contemporary regular script.

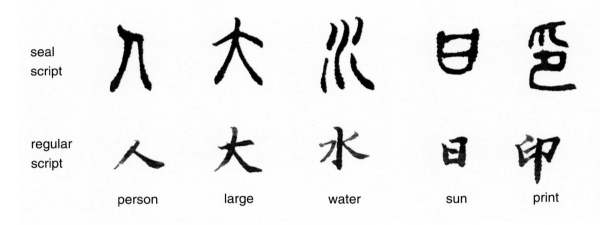

seal script				
regular script				
person	large	water	sun	print

Seal script - regular script comparison (by Wen Jingen)

"Leisure seal" 闲(閑)章

Often the legend on a seal is a person's name, but many Chinese artists like to put something like a saying or a verse in the legend of a seal. Such a seal is called "leisure seal".

Leisure seals: legends reading "Good auspices" (left) and "Luck"

Other tools include paper weights which help keep your paper in place during your execution of a painting, a brush hanger to hang up your washed brush, brush rests to keep your wet brush from touching the table or paper, and **brush rolls** which keep your brushes protected when travelling. A cylindrical **brush container** is often seen on the table of a studio too.

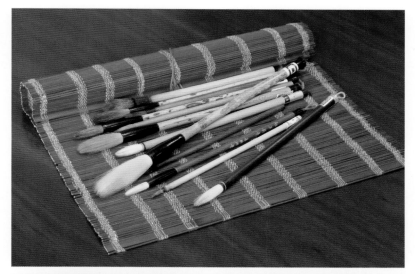

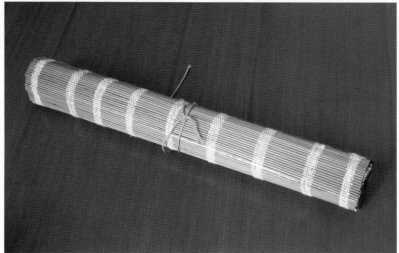

Brush roll, photographs by Wen Jingen

Brushwork and Application of Ink

Brushwork and Ink 笔(筆)墨

Brushwork and ink have been regarded as the most essential elements of Chinese painting. The Chinese judge paintings not only from the images presented in the picture, but from the quality of brushwork and ink application skills. Over centuries, many art theorists and art historians have conducted heated debates over this issue.

Strokes

The uniqueness of Chinese painting lies in its quality of line. Line is also used in Western art — the decoration on Hellenic pottery is marvellously forceful, flowing and rhythmic. Chinese artists apply lines in special ways. They pay much attention to how to begin a line, how to end it, how to move the brush during the execution of a line, how to keep the brush tip in a certain position or change it, and so on. Brushwork in Chinese painting is much the same as in Chinese calligraphy, which has been a very important basic course for Chinese painters. If you know Chinese calligraphy, you will have little difficulty in grasping the brushwork in Chinese painting. If you do not know Chinese calligraphy, you will learn to control the brush while learning to paint.

Control your brush. When summing up his father's experiences in artistic creation, the 11th / 12th century artist Guo Si points out that the artist must control the brush and not be controlled by it; and that one should use ink but not be used by it. Chinese painters have observed this adage over centuries. An artist does not take just any stroke the brush produces, instead, he endeavours to achieve the desired strokes and ink effects.

Holding a Chinese brush may be problematic for a beginner, especially a non-Chinese one. It is not easy to hold the brush steady and produce a robust stroke. How you hold the brush and move it will be discerned in the resulting strokes, just as the way a man walks can be discerned in his footprints. Be patient and practice for a time, and you will learn to control the brush and produce the strokes you desire.

Hold the brush vertically. Chinese calligraphers hold the brush vertically. They use their thumb and all the fingers to hold their brush, with the thumb pressing on one side of the brush shaft, the forefinger holding back, the middle finger reinforcing the forefinger, the ring finger pushing the brush shaft and the little finger reinforcing the ring finger. Leave an empty "cave" in your palm. In other words, do not hold the brush with a fist!

Basically, Chinese painters hold the brush in the same way as Chinese calligraphers. But as there is a greater variety of brushstrokes in painting, Chinese painters use the brush with more variation than Chinese calligraphers — sometimes holding the brush at a slant.

Centre-tip stroke *zhongfeng* 中锋(鋒): Produce a stroke while keeping the brush tip at the centre of the stroke to be produced. In doing such a stroke, one usually holds the brush shaft vertically. This is the main stroke used in Chinese calligraphy. A stroke produced in this way looks full and hefty.

Producing a centre-tip stroke, photograph by Wen Jingen

Centre-tip strokes

Side-tip stroke *cefeng* 侧锋(側鋒): Produce a stroke by keeping the brush tip to one side of the stroke, usually by holding the brush at a slant. This stroke is often avoided in calligraphy, but used in painting. A side-tip stroke can set off the gradation of ink and colour in a stroke. "Flying white" is sometimes left in the end of the stroke which brings out the contrast of dark and pale shades — such strokes accentuate the tactile value of the depicted objects.

Sometimes a stroke is produced by keeping the brush tip touching the paper, while varying the rest of the stroke mark as the brush is moved across the painting.

Forward (pulling) stroke *shunfeng* 顺锋(順鋒) and backward (pushing) stroke *nifeng* 逆锋(鋒). The former is produced by moving the brush away from the brush tip. The latter is produced by moving the brush in the direction against the brush tip.

Side-tip stroke, photograph by Wen Jingen

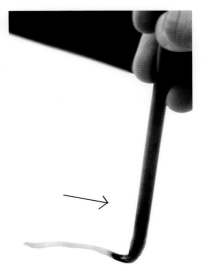

Pulling stroke, Photograph by Wen Jingen

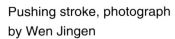

Pushing stroke, photograph by Wen Jingen

Texture-stroke *cunfa* 皴法: Load the brush tip with a little ink or colour and make light strokes to accentuate the surface of rocks, tree trunks, ground or other objects. Usually several layers of such strokes are applied.

Texture stroke

texture strokes

Texture strokes applied on the face, by Wen Jingen

Skimming stroke *cafa* 擦法: Ensure the brush tip contains very little ink or colour (if the brush tip is wet, dry the brush tip by pressing it onto tissue paper or cloth) and skim the brush over the paper. The skimming stroke is even lighter and drier than the texture stroke.

Skimming stroke, by Wen Jingen

Texture strokes and skimming strokes are usually employed to depict the surface of rocks and trees in landscape paintings. Such strokes are also used in figure painting to depict some coarse surfaces.

Dotting. A dot is executed by one touch of the brush tip. Do not touch up. An old, blunt-tipped brush is preferable than a new, sharp-pointed brush. So, do not throw away your used brush.

Move the brush with your wrist — do not move your brush with your fingers, otherwise you will make unsightly, flimsy strokes.

A painting can be produced by using only one kind of stroke, but usually a range of different strokes are employed.

Various dotting strokes, by Wen Jingen

Good brushwork is expressive and forceful.

Uncontoured painting (literally, "boneless painting" *mogu* 没骨画[畫]): You can produce a painting without outlining the subjects. Such a Chinese painting is rather like a watercolour but using ink instead of colour. The contrast between dark and light ink (occasionally with places where the ink or colour is left out) produces a rhythmic effect. You may complete a leaf, flower petal, or anything else in one stroke, and you may also apply several layers of ink or colour, but do not retouch one stroke or dot. You may add another stroke before or after the first mark dries. In ancient times uncontoured paintings were made on sized silk or paper. Nowadays, many artists produce these paintings on unsized paper.

Dancer (depicted without outlining)
by Wen Jingen

Contoured and uncontoured methods may be used in one picture.

In this picture the head and hand are outlined while the clothing is uncontoured.

Writer by Wen Jingen

Skills of applying ink

Ink is more than just a black colour. In Western painting black is an item in a spectrum of colours. Some Impressionists even avoided using black. In Chinese painting, ink is one of the two predominating factors (the other being brushwork). Some art theorists even believe that a painting without proper brushwork and ink application, even though executed by a Chinese artist, cannot be considered "Chinese".

Fragrance in Lotus Pool by Hu Gongshou (1823 — 1886)

In this painting lotus leaves and cattail leaves are depicted in ink. In nature they are green.

Good application of ink should be clear and rhythmic.

Wet-on-wet ink *pòmo* 破墨: Before the first layer of ink is dry, add another stroke. You may add dark ink onto light or add light ink onto dark — you must add the second stroke before the first layer of ink is dry. But if you put the second stroke too soon, the two layers of ink will blend into one bland patch.

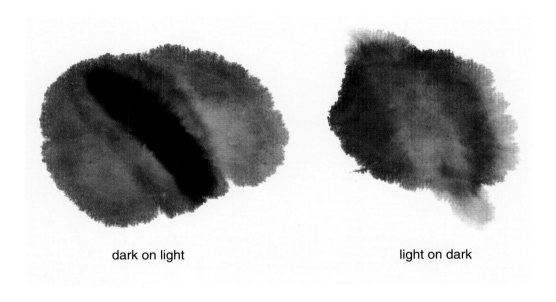

dark on light   light on dark

second touch too early   second touch too late

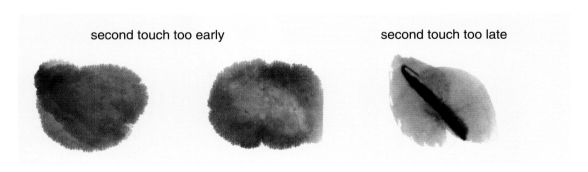

Illustration by Wen Jingen

Accumulated ink *jimo* 积(積)墨: Usually the first layers are in light ink and later layers are in dark ink. Some artists however, repeatedly add layers of ink using a brush with a loosened tip.

Summer Rain by Wang Zhen, 1920
Note the peaks are depicted with accumulated ink.

地行不識名和姓
大江高陽一洞庭
光跫壺宴罷仙淋
漓襟袖尚模糊

Immortal Depicted in Splash-ink by Liang Kai (active 12th — 13th centuries)

Splash-ink *pōmo* 泼(潑)墨: In fact, you do not really splash ink onto paper — just paint with a brush oversaturated with ink to produce broad, uninhibited marks.

In the past some artists splashed ink onto silk to produce a painting!

A historical document says that the painter Wang Qia (died c. AD 805) poured ink onto silk and making use of the tracks of the ink, he turned different shapes of ink marks into trees, water, mountains, rocks, and other objects. It is said he even used his hands and feet to exploit the ink shades. What a playful way of artistic creation!

Splash-colour *pocai* 泼(潑)彩: Some artists apply colour to large areas instead of ink, using a brush oversaturated with paint.

Monster Killer by Wen Jingen

Dried-up ink *jiaomo* 焦墨: If you grind an ink stick on the ink stone for a long time, you will produce a very thick, almost dry liquid. Extremely dark ink produced this way is called dried-up ink. It can be used to depict the pupil of an eye, eyebrows, or some important parts in a picture. Bottled ink does not have this grade of darkness. In that case you have to pour a small amount of bottled ink onto an ink stone and grind an ink stick on it. As a rule, dried-up ink is used sparingly.

Overnight ink *sumo* 宿墨: After leaving for a night, the glue contained in ink will separate and become granules floating in the liquid. Generally, one should avoid using overnight ink. But occasionally, this ink can be used for some special effects.

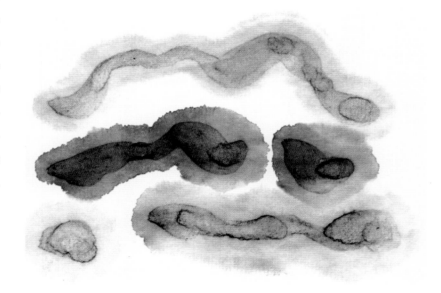

You can also load the brush with different shades of ink or colour.

Illustration by Wen Jingen

Colour

In Chinese ink painting, colour is usually complementary to ink and colours can be mixed with ink. Small patches of pure colour can also be added to highlight some part of a picture.

Mixing colours:

Colours can be divided into the categories of warm colours (red, yellow, purple, ochre, brown) and cool colours (blue, green). White and black are called the "extreme colours". Theoretically, all colours can be obtained by mixing a certain amount of red, yellow and blue, so the three colours are called the "primary colours". Black is the mixture of all three primary colours, but in practice mixing the three primary colours does not produce pure black.

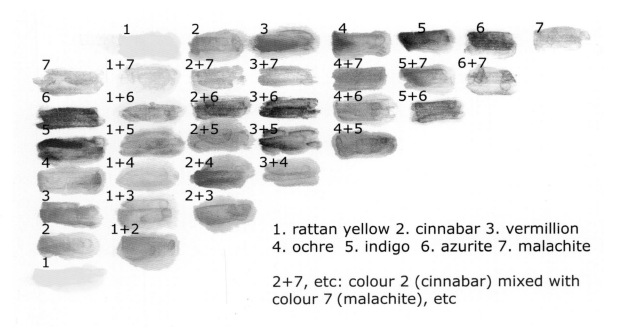

1. rattan yellow 2. cinnabar 3. vermillion
4. ochre 5. indigo 6. azurite 7. malachite

2+7, etc: colour 2 (cinnabar) mixed with colour 7 (malachite), etc

A few of many possibilities. Illustration by Wen Jingen

Mixing colours and ink. Illustration by Wen Jingen

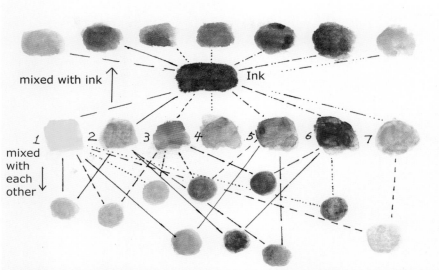

mixed with ink

Ink

mixed with each other

1   2   3   4   5   6   7

1 rattan yellow 2 cinnabar 3 vermillion 4 ochre 5 indigo 6 azurite 7 malachite

Varying the amount of ingredients (in this case, indigo and rattan yellow) produces different shades of colour. Illustration by Wen Jingen

indigo

rattan yellow

When you use mineral colours, make sure the layer of colour is not too thick. The opaque colour will obliterate the ink shades and make the whole picture lack animation. Vegetable colours are transparent and tend to reveal the ink strokes under them. Use more vegetable colours than mineral colours.

Colours can be applied flatly, but in an ink painting, artists usually apply the second layer of colour before the first layer of colour or ink is dry.

Illustration by Wen Jingen

Painting a Face, a Hand and a Foot

We will study facial features separately before we learn to paint the whole face.

The eye and eyebrow

The eye is called the "window to the mind". Well-depicted eyes often reveal a person's mental state and personal character. Eyes in a painting can possess many subtleties. Vividly painted eyes can imbue the whole picture with vitality. An artist must therefore pay great attention to the depiction of eyes.

First, place the eye sockets in the right positions. The distance between the two eyes must be carefully considered. Foreshortening is an important factor that contributes to a realistic representation. If you have studied drawing, you know that the eye is not on a flat surface. It can be broken up into surfaces at different angles.

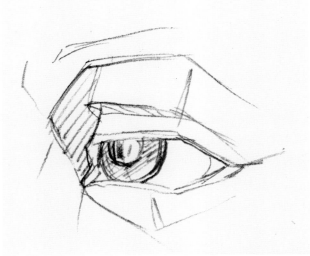

Surfaces on an eye by Wen Jingen

In Chinese painting, artists do not show those angles by strokes as oil painters do, but the brushstrokes should suggest the differing directions of the surfaces. Observe the relative sizes of the eyes and show the transition between different facets. The shape and position of the eyebrows should be measured accurately.

Secondly, paint the sockets, eyeballs and eyelids in light ink strokes — the width of brushstrokes should vary with the rising and receding of the surrounds to the eyes. After this, paint the rims of eyelids and the pupils, and then paint the eyebrows in accordance with the direction of hair on the brows. When this is done, accentuate some parts of the eyelids and eyebrows with extremely dark "dried-up ink". Leave the highlight spot on the pupil and white of the eye unpainted.

Further elaborate the eyelids with dark, light, dry and wet strokes. Set off the structural relationship between the eye and the eyebrow. Emphasis should be given to the different facets in the turnings of the eyebrow. Make the eyeball expressive.

Anecdote: painting in the pupils of dragons' eyes 画龙点睛(畫龍點睛)

It is said the great artist Zhang Senyou (active during the early sixth century) painted four dragons on the walls of a temple. He left the pupils of the eyes unpainted for a long time, saying that with pupils the dragons would fly away. People thought that was ridiculous and insisted. But as the artist started painting the pupils in the eyes, there was peal of thunder and two of the dragons soared up into the clouds. The other two dragons without pupils remained on the walls.

Use different strokes to show the tactile value of the eye and eyebrow. Once the ink is applied, add colour. Apply strokes in light ochre and malachite layer by layer, leaving the highlight spot on the pupil unpainted. When the colour is dry, add eyelashes in dried-up ink. Note that the white of the eye is not really always white — it should be shaded so as to set off the highlight on the pupil.

Flat eye

In this painting the eye (and the whole face) of the monk appears flat, like an eye in ancient Egyptian paintings. The artist did not understand the structure of the face and put the eye on the surface of the temple, parallel to the picture plane instead of the front of the face that was perpendicular to the picture plane.

Monk(detail) by Luo Ping (1733 — 1799)

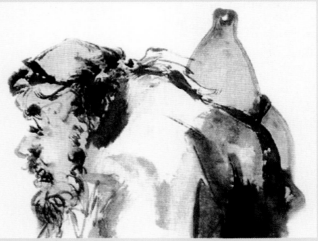

Immortal(detail) by Huang Shen (1687 — 1772)

In this exaggeratedly executed painting the eye was put on the right plane and the head looks three-dimensional.

The nose and ear

The nose and ears are fixed organs on the head. However the nose, being at the centre of the face, is a very prominent feature. The line marking the bridge of the nose plays an important role in determining the direction of the face when the head is turned. A nose may be broad or narrow, high or low. The nose of European people usually has a higher and more pointed bridge than that of Asian people. The nose consists mainly of a bridge and nostrils. An aquiline nose has a beak-formed point. A snub nose has its nostrils exposed outwardly. Different shapes of the nose help to characterise different personalities.

The ear on either side of the head has a complex structure. It has little to do with the facial expression, but its colour may change when one blushes. An ear may be long, floppy, or round. Ears hanging down to the shoulder, an exaggerated depiction used in Chinese art, usually appear on the head of a Buddha or the God of Longevity.

Bodhisatva Guanyin, wall painting in Dunhuang; note his drooping ears (interestingly, later this deity became female and we should say "her ears").

Nose

First observe the overall structure of the nose, its position and direction. Attention must be given to the rising and falling of the line presenting the bridge of the nose, and the structural relationship between the lower nose and nostrils. Contour the nose with light ink in mild yet forceful strokes of various widths.

Surfaces on a nose
by Wen Jingen

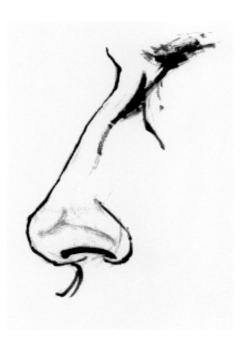

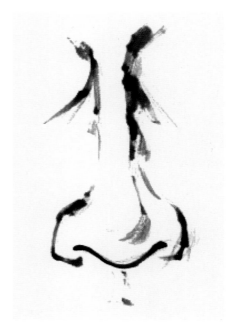

When the outline is done, reinforce the structure of the nose with dark texture and skimming strokes. Then shade the nose with light ink — your strokes should show the tactile value of the soft and hard parts of the nose.

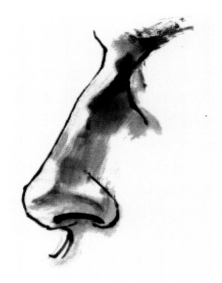

Illustrate the sides of the nose using dry strokes. The tip of the nose should be painted distinctly. Strokes should join up with each other naturally. The depiction of the nose should be harmonious with other features.

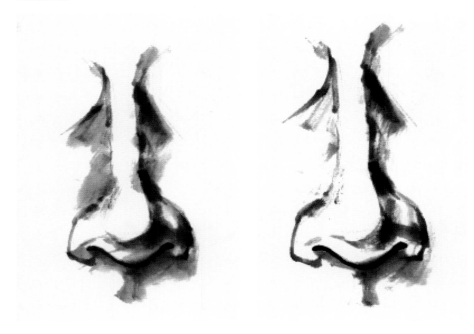

When the ink strokes are complete, add colour using light ochre and malachite. Do not apply the colour flatly, but use various shades, leaving the highlight unpainted. The colour strokes should be in keeping with the planes in different directions. Finally, stress the salient parts with a little dried-up ink.

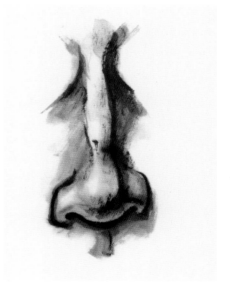

The ear

First, determine the position and overall shape of the ear. Paint its outline with dry strokes in light ink. Carefully show the details, noting that some parts thrust into adjacent areas, while others protrude out. The outline of the ear should match the adjoining areas. Use flexible strokes.

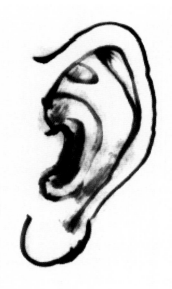

Show the ear details with dark ink. Add texture and skimming strokes in light ink to bring out the structure of the ear, making it look three-dimensional.

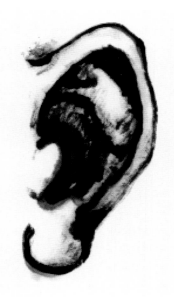

Further elaborate the ear with light ink. Join the ear and the adjacent hair, earlobe and jawbone naturally. Integrate every part into a harmonious whole.

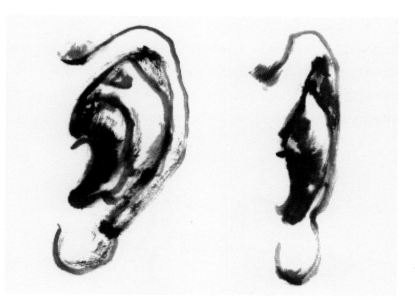

When the ink strokes are done, apply light ochre and malachite. The strokes should be in keeping with the rising and falling of the surface of the ear. The brushstrokes should be rhythmic and varied. Add the final touch in dried-up ink.

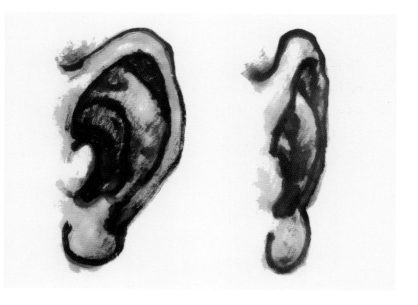

The mouth

The mouth is the most mobile and expressive organ on the face. Structurally it consists of the upper and lower lips, the upper and lower jawbones, and the muscles round the mouth (*orbicularis oris*). Movement of other facial muscles can change the shape of the mouth and thereby show different emotions and feelings.

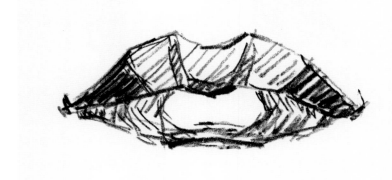

Surfaces on a mouth by Wen Jingen

The variation of the surfaces is noticeable in the mouth. When depicting a mouth, first observe the emotional expression manifested on it. Outline the mouth with light ink strokes. Strokes should be flowing, smooth and natural.

After the outline is done, model the mouth with dark, light, dry and wet ink strokes. The corners of the mouth should be accurately depicted. Bring out the subtle expression of the mouth, and show the line between the upper and lower lips precisely. As a rule, the lower part of the lower lip is darker. Contrast of light and dark strokes helps to model the mouth.

Accentuate the turning of the lines that represent the upper and lower lips. These lines should underline the volume of the lips in the correct perspective. Try to achieve an overall effect.

When ink strokes are finished, add ochre and malachite mixed with a little vermilion as light colour. If you put too much dark colour on the picture, you will have no way to amend it. It is better to apply several layers of light colour than one layer of strong colour. Final dry strokes in dark ink will bring out a whole-some picture of the mouth.

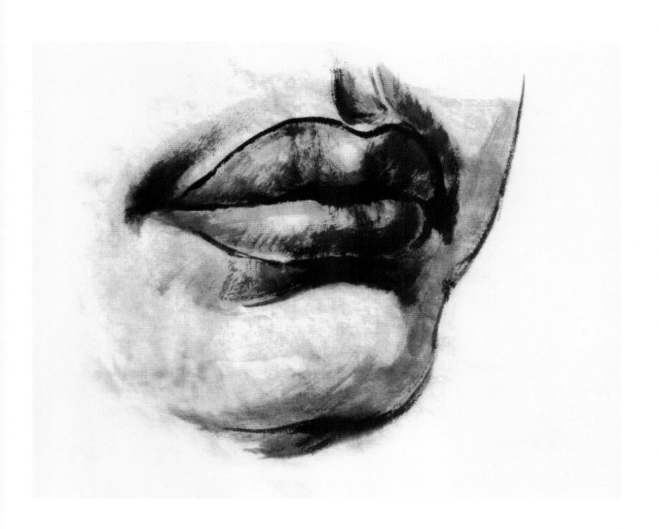

Hair

People of different ages, gender and occupations have different hairstyles. The countless styles fall into categories of long, short, ancient and modern hairdos. Hairstyle betrays a person's aesthetic taste, personal character, occupation and social status.

In depicting hair, close attention should be paid to the overall shape and structure. Employ both lax and lively strokes. A certain amount of exaggeration is preferable. The beginning, movement and end of the stroke should be spontaneous. The direction of strokes should help to indicate the root and end of each hair. At the same time, the hair and the face should be linked naturally. Side-tip strokes in dark and light ink are usually employed — it is better to apply ink in rhythmic shades.

When the ink marks are completely dry, add light indigo to show tufts and wisps of hair in a better relief. The brushstrokes should not be too mechanical. Leave some space unpainted. Finally, add light ink at the temples and the edge of hair until the hair and the face shade into each other.

Beard

The beard as a symbol of age, male gender and also a sign of a certain personality often appears in paintings of middle-aged or old men and in ancient figure paintings. A beard can also reveal a man's occupation, temperament, and education.

When you paint a beard, try to find out its characteristic and group the individual hairs into tufts. Show the overall structure of the beard with light ink. Brushstrokes should underline the resilience of the beard. Texture-strokes may be used and you may also use the technique of painting details of the hair. Do not colour the entire beard — leave some part unpainted.

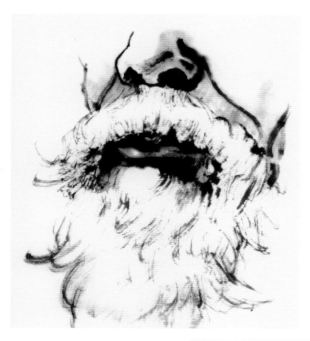

The cheek

People of different races have different hues on their cheeks. The yellow person's cheeks can be coloured with ochre and malachite, and in painting the cheek of a woman or child, a little yellow or vermilion may be added. The white skinned woman has rosy cheeks which may be painted with vermilion, malachite and indigo. A black person's cheeks may be painted in brown mixed with ink. Black people of certain ethnic groups have cheeks with a blue or brown tint. Accordingly, indigo or ochre can be used. Artists usually paint the cheek in the following steps.

1. You may use charcoal to do the draft. When the painting is finished, you may wipe off the charcoal with a piece of cloth. Do the outline with ink strokes. To leave an opportunity for correction, beginners may outline in extreme pale ink first, followed by an outline in dark ink. If the cheek is of an aged person, depict the wrinkles on the cheeks with texture-strokes and, if necessary, skimming strokes. Shade the cheek with light ink.

2. Add a bit of indigo to the recesses of wrinkles.

3. Apply colour on the cheekbone. You may leave the highlight unpainted. Alternatively, in the traditional way, you may add a darker colour on the cheekbone than in other places. This is because the local colour on the cheekbone is redder than elsewhere. Before the first layer is dry, put on another layer.

4. Add the final touch.

A new way for painting cheeks:

Step 1

Step 2

Step 3

Step 4

Step 5

Illustrations by Wen Jingen   Step 6

King, Queen and Minister, mural from Kizil Caves, Xinjiang, 7th — 10th centuries

Note the recession is shaded.

A traditional way for painting cheeks:

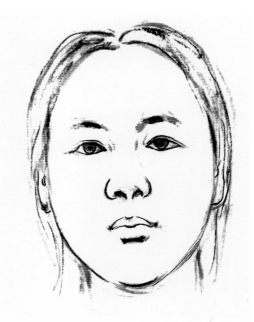

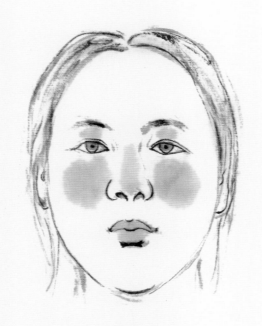

no highlight on the cheekbones

Illustrations by Wen Jingen

You have studied how to paint features of a face. When you produce a figure painting or portrait, do not finish the features one by one. Instead, it is better that you paint the whole face step by step. Outline the whole face, apply the strokes on all features, shade them, and add colour to them. In short, you must not only see trees but the whole forest as well. Read more about painting a whole face on p. 138.

Beauty by unknown artist, AD 704

Note the cheekbone is shaded.

The hand and foot

The hand

The hand is a very important organ on the human body. A hand in different positions and movements can be in a great variety of shapes. Chinese artists have a saying, "The hand is the most difficult part in painting a human figure." To have a good understanding of the hand, you must study its anatomic structure, paying special attention to the relationship between the palm and fingers. Observe the hand in various gestures from different angles.

First paint the outline of the hand with light ink. Close attention should be paid to the joints on fingers and between the palm and fingers.

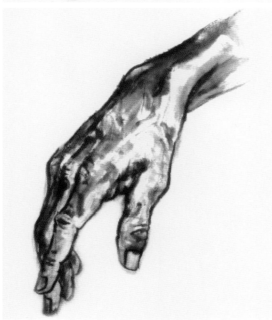

Apply dark and light strokes to model the whole hand. Texture and skimming strokes can be used if necessary. Stress the tactile value of bones and muscles.

Elaborate on detail. The hand and wrist should be carefully joined so that the hand looks as if it is "growing" from the wrist. The ink should be in different shades. The dark and the light strokes should be in sharp contrast. Use dry marks in light ink to link the different shades.

After the ink marks are done, apply colour with a medium-sized brush. Please note that the colours on the back of the hand and on the palm have different hues. The final strokes can be applied in dried-up ink.

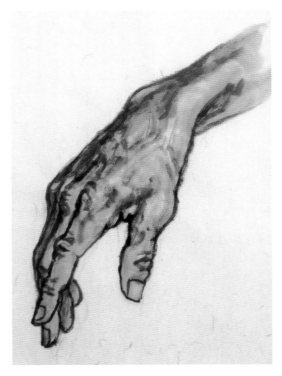

The foot

Though the foot has fewer variations of movement, it makes an essential contribution to the painting. For example, an old man sitting cross-legged and smoking a pipe with his thumb raised looks to be enjoying himself at leisure. A village boy paddling in a stream brings out a mischievous air.

Anatomically, a foot consists of the ankle, heel, sole, instep and toes. A foot is usually depicted together with a length of the leg. Understanding the correlation of the ankles, shin and fibula is very important in producing a realistic picture of the foot.

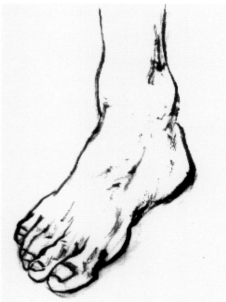

First, paint the outline of the foot with dry strokes in light ink. Apply side-tip strokes to shade the surfaces of the arch and toes.

Elaborate on the details of the foot with dark and light ink marks. The overall relation between the heel, the instep and the ankle must be correct. Ink should be in different shades.

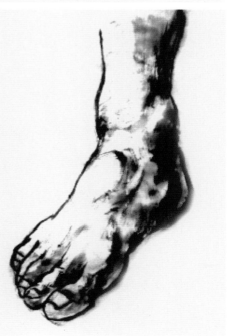

Finally, add colour. It is better to apply light colour several times than to apply strong colour once. The final strokes can be in dried-up ink. The finished picture of a foot should look steady and in motion. A young man's feet will show the joints of bones protruding in an obvious manner, so the strokes must be bold, distinct and vigorous. An old man's feet have a weather-beaten surface, so dry, texture and skimming strokes can be employed. Women and children's feet have a tender surface, the brushwork should be smooth and flowing, the strokes should be wet and in a ruddy colour.

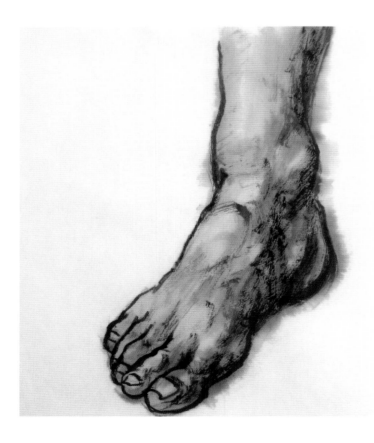

Factors for Lifelike Depiction

Since ancient times, many Chinese artists have striven to achieve a resemblance of the spirit of life in their art. Achieving both vividness and formal likeness (*shen xing jian bei* 神形兼备[備]) has been the utmost objective pursued by Chinese artists.

The human eye does not work the same way as the lens in a camera. It sees what the human head can understand. Only Impressionists "see" the spectrum of light. You cannot catch the same rich spectrum in colour photography despite the sophistication of modern cameras. Where the Western artists "see" light and colour, Chinese painters mainly "see" the line and ink shades.

However, the basic elements for a lifelike depiction for Chinese and Western artists are the same. Therefore, the basic knowledge (anatomy and perspective) and training (drawing) for Chinese figure paintings are the same as those for students of painting in the West. If you have never read about anatomy and perspective, I strongly recommend that you read books on these subjects. In this book, only rough guidelines will be given concerning proportions of the human body.

Proportions

"To work away at a canon of masculine and feminine proportions to seek the variations out of which character arises, to examine more closely the anatomical structure, and to seek the beautiful forms that mean exterior perfection - to such difficult researches I wish you to contribute your share just as I, for my part, have made some preliminary investigations". — Goethe

The head

A front of the head looks like an egg standing on its small end. Chinese artists divide a head into three equal parts from the top to chin and five parts from the end of one ear to the other. For European artists the traditional rules of proportion show the face divided six equal squares, two by three. The different approaches only show that neither of them is absolutely accurate. They just serve as a rough guide.

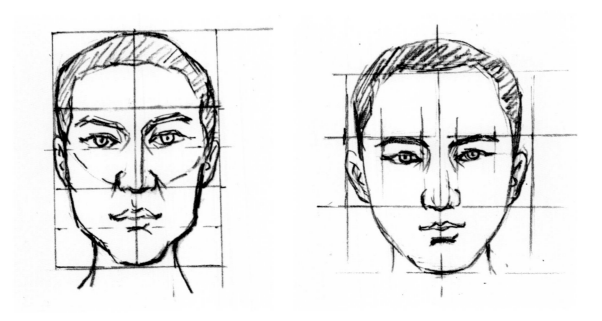

Illustration by Wen Jingen

Imagining a box to contain the head will help you to arrange it in correct perspective.

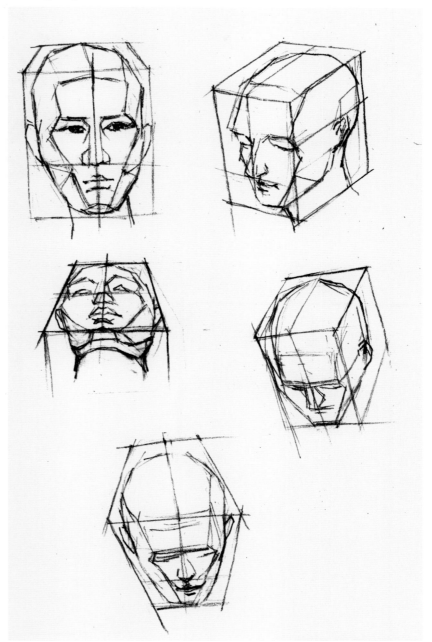

Illustration by Wen Jingen

Byzantine artists used a three-circle scheme for depiction of the head. To today's viewers, it is ridiculously inaccurate and highly schemetised.

Chinese sculptors of Esoteric Buddha statues worked strictly according to the standardised measurement defined in the book *The Manual of Measurement for Creating Images* (*Zao Xiang Duliang Jing* 造像度量经) published in 1742. The measurement is not an objective reflection of the human form either.

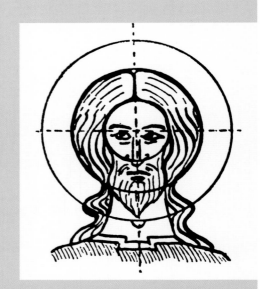

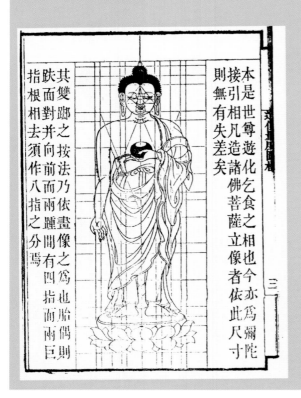

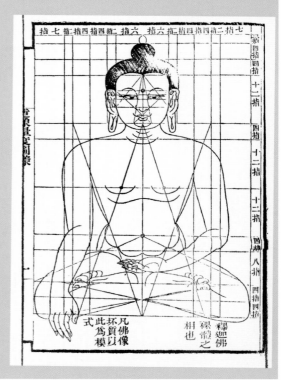

The body

European artists in figure drawing or painting use proportions that an average person is seven and half heads tall (including the head), an ideal figure, eight heads tall, and heroic figure (gods or supermen), eight and half heads tall. Chinese artists have an old formula that the height of a standing person is seven times his head, that of a sitting human, five times the head, and that of a human sitting with his legs crossed, three and half times the head. A hand measured from the tip of the middle finger to the wrist is two-thirds the height of the head. The length of the foot is the same as the height of the head. The above however are only guidelines. Proportions differ from person to person and also change with age, race and pose. This rough guide only helps the beginner to avoid severely disproportioned images.

Measure your model with your eyes. You should also remember that a person is not a flat piece. In certain perspectives some parts may be enlarged and others reduced in size (it does a figure painter good to read a book on perspective.). Look at the illustration. — the girl's hands are of equal size when they are at the plane parallel to the picture plane.

When she extends one hand forward and the other backward, the hand closer to the picture plane looks larger than the other.

More importantly, in a half or three-quarter view, some parts may be foreshortened. Conceive a human body as a series of solids and you will achieve the correct foreshortening more easily.

Photograph by Wen Jingen

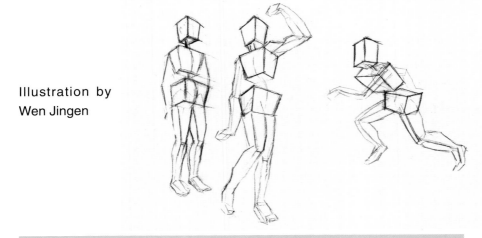

Illustration by
Wen Jingen

Figure (detail) by Huang Shen (1687 — 1772)

Being ignorant of anatomy and perspective, some ancient Chinese
painters painted awkward images of a raised head.

Drawing a human figure

Early in the 20th century many Chinese art schools adopted the curriculum of the Western art colleges. Drawing has been acknowledged as the most important basic training.

Chinese painters draw human figures in much the same way as Western artists except that the Chinese pay more attention to lines than tonality. You may use a pencil, a pen or charcoal. Before you put your pencil on paper, carry out an overall observation of your model. You will not only pay attention to his or her physical features and proportion, you should also pay attention to his or her occupational characteristics, temperament and mentality as well. In short, your painting of each model should be unique.

Likeness and unlikeness 似与(與)不似之间(間)

Whether likeness is the yardstick for a successful painting has been debated in China for centuries. The great master Qi Baishi (1864 — 1957) held that a masterwork is somewhere between likeness and unlikeness. In his opinion, an exact likeness catered to vulgar taste and an utter unlikeness deceived the viewer.

Rene Berger has a similar view: "At the limit of naturalistic description is rubbish and at the limit of abstraction is nothingness." (Rene Berger, *The Language of Art*, tr. from French by Rihchard James, Thames & Hudson, London, 1963, p. 139)

Because you are preparing for a Chinese painting, you should visualise the effect of your strokes in your future painting while you do a drawing. Imagine which brush strokes will be "converted" from your pencil strokes. Use various lines for different parts of a human body. As for the light in your studio, when you study the anatomic structure of a human body, use bright light so that the contrast of light and shade will throw the anatomic structure into bold relief. But when you paint a picture, it is better to use mild light to avoid sharp contrast of light and shade, because in Chinese painting the contrast of light and dark is not strong.

Sketch by Wen Jingen

Sketching from life and from memory

Apart from drawing, sketching from life and from memory has been the basic training for Chinese painters. To capture an image with your eyes is not the same thing as capturing an image with a camera. The camera can only record what it "sees" while an artist draws what he recognises, understands and keeps in memory. An artist's image is usually simpler, more generalised and more expressive than life. Tools for sketching are simple — you need just a sketchbook and a pen, pencils, charcoal or brushes.

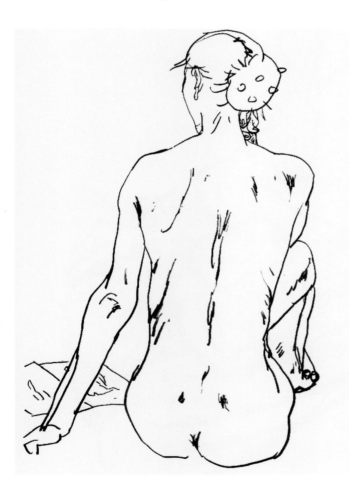

Do not sketch hastily. Observe your model for some time before you put your pencil onto the paper. While you study the proportions of your model, use what you have learned from the course on anatomy. The proportions of the facial features are of crucial importance in doing a realistic picture. Always pay close attention to the overall posture of your model. You will benefit from sketching the details like the head, a hand and a foot.

　　As you make progress, you will learn to sketch confidently. Do lifelike pictures that not only are true to life, but also convey the emotion, mentality and temperament of the model.

However quickly you sketch, you cannot catch some movements with your hand. You have to record such movements with your head. Try to memorise them and when you return home, try to draw them from your memory. This is a very important training. The more images you store in your memory, the better you will paint. In doing a sketch from your memory, begin with the general position of the model. Try to recapture what you have seen from life — your memory may be incomplete. You can supplement your sketch with what you have learned from your homework.

The more you sketch from your memory, the stronger your visual memory will be.

Folds of clothes

Folds of clothes are determined by the human body underneath them. They vary with the postures the model strikes. Also, various fabrics will produce different folds. Lifelike depiction of folds of clothes will make your picture more expressive and meaningful. When you study the folds of your model's attire, you must "see" the human body under the clothes, do not let complicated folds lead your eyes astray. The line indicating the motion of the model (i. e. line of action) must be clear and everything in the painting must be arranged in accordance with that line.

Line of action. Illustration by Wen Jingen

Omit some insignificant lines and stress the lines that are visually beautiful.

Painting a nude and dressing it

An anecdote goes that once a famous 14th century painter was painting a mural. He found it difficult to make the limbs in correct sizes. He treated a friend to a dinner and asked for his advice. His friend said, "Paint a nude figure and then put clothing on it". The painter executed his painting accordingly and sure enough, it was a success.

Loose or tight, broad or clinging to the human body, thick or thin, clothes made of fine or crude fabric give rise to bulky or fine lines that are tightly crowded or widely spaced. Make the folds of your attire vary imposingly.

Silk, gauze, cotton fabrics, synthetic fabrics and leathers are depicted with differing brushwork and ink skills.

If the attire is made of fine and flimsy fabric, the lines you use to depict the folds should be thin and light.

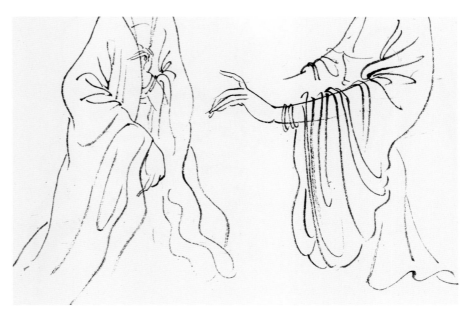

Leather clothes are stiff. Use texture-strokes and skimming strokes to set off their tactile values. Do not forget to leave highlight unpainted.

Hemp and cotton fabrics are crude and heavy. To depict such fabrics you can use dry brushstrokes with a loosened brush tip.

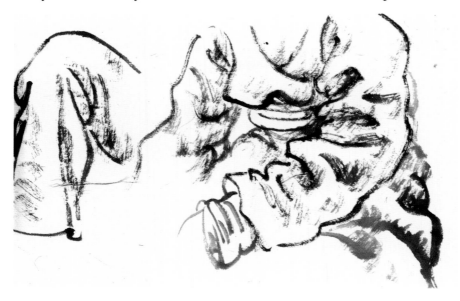

In doing a picture of a clothed person, various brushstrokes, ink spots, wet-on-wet ink, wet and dry strokes plus dried-up ink can be employed.

Painting a portrait

Before you paint, you must study your sitter from the general view. Talk with your model until he or she is relaxed, so that they will look his or her "usual self". Only when they are in such a state of mind, can you produce a picture true to their expression and temperament. For a beginner, a portrait may take three or four hours to finish. When you are familiar with the brushwork and ink, you may complete a portrait in no more than one hour. The A4 or A3 sheet of paper will be fine. Study the different characteristics of male, female, young or old sitters and try to use different brushwork and ink skills to present the nuances in their skin.

Eight types of human faces
Chinese artists categorise human faces in eight types and compare them with eight Chinese characters. They are: 田，甲，由，申，国(國), 目，风(風) and 用

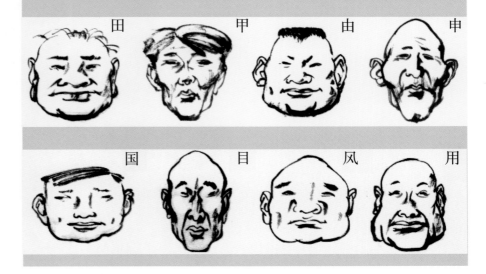

Human facial expressions are infinitely rich and subtle — through constant practice can you hone your skills in showing these.

Step 1: Choose a good position. First of all, determine the angle and position of your sitter's head. Draw the outline with charcoal (when the painting is inked and dry, you can remove any stray charcoal marks with a piece of soft cloth). Mark the proportions with long, straight lines. When this is done, outline the head with a brush in light ink. Do not go into details at this stage.

Step 2: Elaborate your painting with dark ink strokes. Accurately paint the facial features with correct proportions and foreshortening. The lines at joints should be forceful. Different shades of ink should be applied. When the ink is dry, apply texture-strokes in dark ink to accentuate the volume and different surfaces of the features. Cheekbones and lower jawbones should be linked with muscles. Model the muscles around the eyes, lips and gums with texture-strokes. When you put your brush on the paper, use your mind to comprehend the physical structure of the face of your sitter.

Step 3: Colour the portrait. When the ink strokes are completed, add colour to the painting. A yellow person's skin is coloured with ochre, malachite and cinnabar. Mix ochre with a little malachite (do not use too much malachite lest the colour becomes opaque). A white person's skin is tinted with more carmine or scarlet. A black person's skin may be coloured with ochre mixed with ink. — You need not memorise these "recipes". Judge the colour with your own eyes. Besides, even within the same race, nuances in hues exist from person to person. The colour should be clean and transparent. On important parts you may add several layers of colour. Your shading should go with the structure of the depicted object. When you colour the skin under the hair, add some indigo in your colour. The hair should appear as a mass and not a flat piece. Sometimes leaving some parts unpainted is preferable. Again, repeated coating of light, transparent colour is better than one coat of strong colour.

Step 4: Before the first layer of colour is completely dry, cover the whole face with a coat of colour. This coating is mixed using ochre, malachite and a little cinnabar. Add a little rouge on the lips. Bring out different surfaces of the features with different tones and colours. Let your marks shade into each other. Do not leave hard edges on your strokes. Highlights on the nose and lips should be left blank.

Step 5: Final touch. When the colour is dry, use some final strokes to make the whole picture more impressive. If your model's skin colour is dark, you may add some ochre on the back of the paper. When the colour is right, redo the pupils of eyes with dark ink. To stress the tufts of hair, dried-up ink strokes may be added. The upper eyelids, eyebrows, the tip of the nose, and the lips may be reinforced with dried-up ink until the portrait is lifelike and vivid.

The head and hands are the most important parts for a portrait. Spend more time in studying them. When doing a portrait, close attention must be paid to the anatomic proportions, the centre of gravity and the overall posture of the model. Conceive proper strokes and ink shades to achieve desired result. When you view your model, you must analyse it in light of perspective.

Steps to paint a white woman. (Illustrations for white and black people done by Wen Jingen)

1. Outline with charcoal. When your painting is finished, you may wipe off the charcoal traces with a piece of soft cloth. (This is the advantage of charcoal over pencil.) Pay more attention to the model's physiognomic feature than his or her skin colour. You should also note that not all white people are equally white. Some white people may look no less black than black people or no less yellow than yellow people.

2. Paint with ink.

3. Add colour.

Steps to paint a black person. A black person's skin is not pitch black. It usually has a brownish hue. Black people in different regions have different hues in the skin colour. You need not use dark colours. The physiognomic feature is more important than the colour. Even if your picture is not coloured, your model should look "black".

Creating a Figure Painting

To create figure paintings, an artist must draw profusely from life. The artist must see life with an artist's eye and learn to find beauty in common things.

乙酉繊夏於太行山甘泉寶向國盡

Conceiving a painting

Choosing a theme for your painting is very important. Just as the Chinese literary giant Lu Xun (1881-1936) said, one must "select themes with strict criteria and delve into it deeply." Not everything in life is a good motif for a painting. Some subjects are for music, others for poetry, still others for films, and so on. Only when you present a motif that is suitable for painting, can you create a successful work.

When you paint a figure, you should also observe what is around him or her. A good figure painting with well-depicted background will arouse imagination in the viewer's mind. For example, in the painting "Autumn Contemplation" (p. 152), the withering plants in the background suggest the season. The brown lotus pod in the girl's hand and withered lotus behind her imply that her youth is passing away with the elapse of time, like the lotus that has passed its blooming season.

Composition

The visual image in a painting is still. Arranging the objects in the painting in a suggestive and beautiful manner is of crucial importance. The form of a painting is not a realistic recording of life, but a conceived arrangement of pictorial elements.

Take the painting "Autumn Contemplation" for an example. First, you must decide on the posture of the model and her position in the painting. If the paper is square, it is better to put her in the right or left of the painting, not far away from the centre. If you put her exactly at the centre, the painting will look stiff and rigid. But if you put her too far away from the centre, the painting will lose its balance. Paint her in a sitting position, because a seated figure suggests a tranquil visual effect and therefore suits the painting's theme. Her attire should be plain and not too brightly coloured. The plain dress, the sitting position and the milieu make a harmonious unity. The withered lotus flower in her hand is a metaphor for life. Withered plants pose a contrast between the inner world of the subject and the nature.

While you contemplate your picture, you may make sketches on small sheets of paper. Try to present your subject in different angles and choose the best one among them. Once you decide the composition, enlarge it onto a larger sheet of paper. Chinese artists often use charcoal to make rough contour. At this stage details may be omitted.

Applying ink and colour

You have learned how to apply ink and colour to a portrait in previous chapters. In producing a creative figure painting with a meaningful theme, you can apply the same techniques. However, you may wish to achieve the maximum effect of your brushwork, ink and colour application. The creation of an artwork is not just an addition of its technical components. Just as a violinist must know where he should play the lingering sound and where to play a staccato, a painter must deliberate where colour should be highlighted and where it should be subdued. Take the "Autumn Contemplation" again. According the season and the girl's age and mentality, a bright colour is not right. The theme of the painting suggests white for her jacket, because it is a pure, tranquillising colour and strikes a contrast with the background. In choosing a colour for her trousers, I considered grey, brown and black. But I cannot use brown for her trousers, because the lotus pod in her hand is brown. If her trousers are brown too, the colour of the lotus pod and the trousers will blend. Suppose the trousers are grey, what will be the colour for the stones in the background? Black, white or grey? Black stones are rare. If I paint the stone in grey, how shall I make it bounce off from the background? Finally I painted the stone with dark ink. Thus two "extreme colours" (white and black) are used in the subject, bringing it out from the backdrop and at the same time, the grey stone forms a transition between the subject and the background.

When you apply ink strokes you must have the whole painting in your mind. The ink should be in different shades and the colour should be transparent. The layer of colour should not be thick as a heavy coat of mineral pigments or it will cover the ink line.

Finishing the painting

When everything is done, you still need to put the final touch to your painting. You may like to have stronger contrast of ink shades and colours in some parts by adding dark and dried-up ink dots and texture strokes. While executing a painting, spend more time in thinking than painting. In the four years when Leonardo da Vinci created his *Mona Liza*, he did not always work with his brush on the canvas. Instead, he must have spent more time in thinking than in painting.

Inscribing and placing a seal on your painting

Most Chinese artists like to add inscriptions and seal impressions on their paintings. If you like, you can follow suit.

Before the 11th century, Chinese artists seldom put inscriptions on their paintings. Since then, with the rise of the literati painting, scholar-artists developed an interest in writing poems or a prose comment on their works. Placement of the inscriptions is of some importance. An inscription in the right place will help to keep the composition in balance. Seal imprints may have this function too.

Some seals have legends in intaglio while others have legends in relief. The seal legends may be your name, style name or even a saying.

Gallery of Figure Paintings in Ink

Realistic figure paintings

康巴美女 就去邪之不躍志而一瞥，我就被她深々地吸引住了，不离不弃，以為她们善花瓶她和一样拥有知识和智慧以及她们的追求。甲申仲夏作康巴美女寅問國

乙酉年夏月

畫付茂林珎

於太行山甘泉村

賈向國

Exaggeration

相對無語 甲申藏 何國圖畫

Experimental figure paintings

Such paintings have some elements of avant garde art.

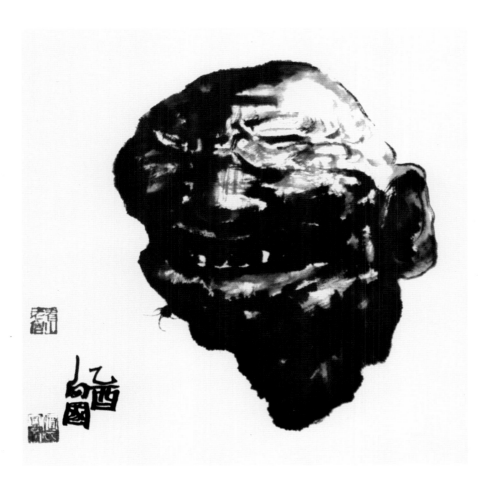

Appendix

DIY: Minimum Backing Makes Your Painting Look Better

Before backing

After backing

Pig Keeper by Wen Jingen

When dry, your painting may be warped. For sophisticated backing and framing you may go to Chinese painting mounters. You can do a minimal backing by yourself at home. First, prepare a thin paste by mixing lukewarm water with wheat flour (or better still, starch) and then pour boiling water into the mixture while stirring it. Alternatively, you can cook the water-flour mixture until it is thick. Dilute the paste by adding cold water little by little, stirring all the time. Place your work face down, flat, on a clean table or glass surface and lightly spray clean water onto the back of your painting. Brush thin paste onto your work, lower another piece of unsized painting paper onto the top of it,

Your creased painting

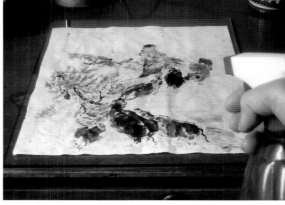
Put it on clean glass or a table surface and spray lightly

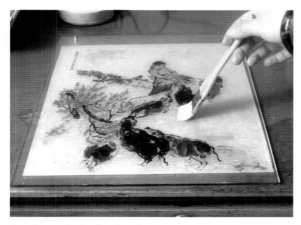
Apply paste to the back

Lower another piece of paper on top

brush out and leave it two or three days to dry. When dry, remove it from the table or glass. To prevent the ink and colour on your paper from running (some bottled ink and tube colours may run when wet), you should wrap your work in a towel, put it in a steamer and steam for 20 minutes before you back it.

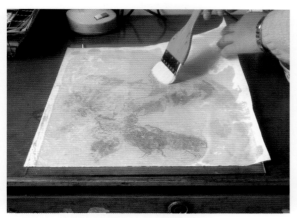
Smooth out creases

Leave it a few days to dry

When dry, cut one side

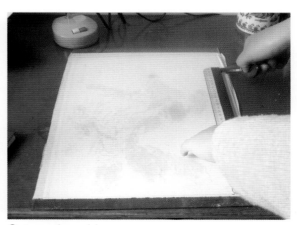
Cut another side

Lift up a corner

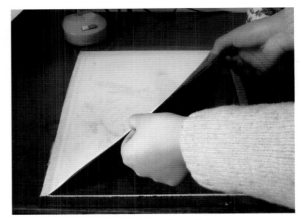

Lift the picture away from the table

Wow

Illustrations for backing by Wen Jingen

图书在版编目（CIP）数据

怎样画人物画 / 贾向国编著，温晋根编译.
－北京: 外文出版社, 2007
（怎样做系列）
ISBN 978-7-119-04813-0

I. 怎... II. 贾... III. 人物画—技法(美术) — 英文 IV. J212.25

中国版本图书馆 CIP 数据核字（2007）第 054217 号

责任编辑　温晋根
封面设计　蔡　荣
插图绘制　贾向国　温晋根　孙树明
策　　划　王贤春　李振国　肖晓明　温晋根

外文出版社网址:
http://www.flp.com.cn
外文出版社电子信箱:
info@flp.com.cn
sales@flp.com.cn

怎样画人物画

贾向国　著

*

© 外文出版社
外文出版社出版
（中国北京百万庄大街 24 号
邮政编码　100037）
北京雷杰印刷有限公司印刷
中国国际图书贸易总公司发行
（中国北京车公庄西路 35 号
北京邮政信箱第 399 号　邮政编码　100044)
2007 年(16 开)第 1 版
2007 年第 1 版第 1 次印刷
（英）
ISBN　978-7-119-04813-0
14000(平)
7-E-3758P